LIONS

alex kuskowski

Consulting Editor, Diane Craig,
M.A./Reading Specialist

Sandcastle

An Imprint of Abdo Publishing
www.abdopublishing.com

visit us at www.abdopublishing.com

Published by Abdo Publishing, a division of ABDO, PO Box 398166, Minneapolis, Minnesota 55439.
Copyright © 2015 by Abdo Consulting Group, Inc. International copyrights reserved in all countries.
No part of this book may be reproduced in any form without written permission from the publisher.
SandCastle™ is a trademark and logo of Abdo Publishing.

Printed in the United States of America, North Mankato, Minnesota
062014
092014

THIS BOOK CONTAINS
RECYCLED MATERIALS

Editor: Liz Salzmann
Content Developer: Nancy Tuminelly
Cover and Interior Design: Anders Hanson, Mighty Media, Inc.
Photo Credits: Shutterstock

Library of Congress Cataloging-in-Publication Data
Kuskowski, Alex., author.
  Lions / Alex Kuskowski.
     pages cm. -- (Zoo animals)
  Audience: 004-009.
  ISBN 978-1-62403-272-1
  1. Lion--Juvenile literature. I. Title.
  QL737.C23K875 2015
  599.757--dc23

                        2013041400

SandCastle™ Level: Transitional

SandCastle™ books are created by a team of professional educators, reading specialists, and content developers
around five essential components—phonemic awareness, phonics, vocabulary, text comprehension, and fluency—to
assist young readers as they develop reading skills and strategies and increase their general knowledge. All books
are written, reviewed, and leveled for guided reading, early reading intervention, and Accelerated Reader® programs
for use in shared, guided, and independent reading and writing activities to support a balanced approach to literacy
instruction. The SandCastle™ series has four levels that correspond to early literacy development. The levels are
provided to help teachers and parents select appropriate books for young readers.

EMERGING · BEGINNING · **TRANSITIONAL** · FLUENT

CONTENTS

LIONS

Lions are big cats.

They are from **Asia** and **Africa**.

People see lions at the zoo.

AT THE ZOO

Lions at the zoo live in a pen. They have trees. They have water.

LION FEATURES

Male lions have manes.
The mane grows
around the lion's neck.

Lions live in a group. A group of lions is called a pride.

Lions make a lot of noise.
They hiss, **purr**, and roar.
They make noise to
communicate.

FOOD

In the wild, lions hunt for food. At zoos, lions are given meat to eat.

LION CUBS

Young lions are called cubs. Cubs live with their mothers for two years.

LION FUN

Cubs play together. They practice hunting.

Lions lay around.
They rest up to
20 hours a day.

FAST FACTS

- Lions have the loudest roar of all big cats.

- Lion cubs are born with spots. The spots fade as they grow.

- The **Swahili** word for lion is "simba."

- **Asian** lions are smaller than **African** lions.

QUICK QUIZ

1. Lions live in a pride.
   True or False?

2. **Female** lions have manes.
   True or False?

3. Lions roar to **communicate**.
   True or False?

4. Lions never lay around.
   True or False?

GLOSSARY

Africa - the second largest continent. Kenya, Egypt, and Senegal are in Africa.

Asia - the largest of the continents. Russia, India, and China are in Asia.

communicate - to share ideas, information, or feelings.

female - being of the sex that can produce eggs or give birth. Mothers are female.

male - being of the sex that can father babies. Fathers are male.

purr - to make a low, soft sound in your throat.

Swahili - a language spoken by many people in Africa.